THE SHAPE OF A WOMAN

Jane -

Thought you'd enjoy this newly published book by our dear friend Kathleen ☺

Love you -

B & D

brikksen.com

For Jane,

THE SHAPE OF A WOMAN

POEMS

All the best!

KATHLEEN WILLOUGHBY

Kathleen Willoughby

Keep the Voice

Published by Keep the Voice, LLC, under exclusive license

ISBN-13: 978-1-966039-05-1

"Future Forecast" was included in *Only in Florida! An Anthology to Benefit the W. T. Bland Public Library of Mount Dora, Florida,* published by Keep the Voice, LLC

Cover design by Stacy Thomas Smith

Cover painting: *The Shape of a Woman* by Kathleen Willoughby

For Linda, the
demanding muse,
and Bill, the poetry
whisperer

THE SHAPE OF A WOMAN

One

Two

Three

Four

Five

Six

One

The Inconstant Poet

And when the guests
have gone at last, taking their
suitcases and memories,
the poem returns
like a sullen lover, no longer
banished to a foreign land.

Two

The Beginning of the Poem, or Love

(after Neruda)

I miss you, as I miss the kiss
of the crow upon my shoulder.
I want you, as I want the poppies
who show their bloodied
faces to me alone.
I love you as a small child
loves the world; exploring
the unknown with awe.
I long for you, and only you,
my song. In my sleep, I find you
with no words. Come closer.
I will name you.

Emily's Pleasures

I am a passionate gardener.
No lover's touch, but this:
the lilac scent of earthy bloom
when windows are splayed
wide open to wild delights
of a night in early June.

I compose a quiet scene
in which I come fragrant
to your moon-drunk room.
No, no. I must imagine
a fresh unfolding for the
flower-poem that is you.

Stronger than spring's early kiss
of star-faced daffodil's innocence;
or the tulip's tremulous opening,
I seek the violent heat of summer's
fast bloom and chaotic loosening. Yes.

But look at all that undoing:
the thunderstorms and reckless ruin—
those trampled roses in our path—
petals crushed to bruised perfumes.

Let's decant the lilac to sip
at our leisure. We have time.
We'll untangle the vines
of future pleasures: a fine occupation.

A brief hesitation, no longer
than it takes to—
Oh, and how suddenly
this bouquet of you
is love’s last gift—
to harvest. To taste. To recall.

Our Song

I love a woman who loves words;
who plucks them, ripening, one by one

from a private vine
of her own making. She strips

fattened fruit with studied care,
bites, and holds.

I bite back hard, bruising open lips
in my desire to feel sound in flesh.

No sacrifice this, we swallow everything whole,
twisting language until it gives.

Some Gin Joint

You slipped in through a side door:
the dull barstool and wooden floor
streaked with pomegranate stain.

A bright flash of yellow—
Prothonotary warbler—and just like that,
Spring wings into those lost last nights.

A thousand flickering stars
light up this dive bar, where you are
a tiny paper umbrella, an origami
of delight, a fleeting joy to savor.

Sweet bird, you are nothing like
the karaoke performers in drunken sync.
Your songs are a giving forth; a pleasing
thrumming in an ancient tongue.

Teach me a new escape; help me
to clear this space. Give me
the scent of juniper, the shush
of pines and green release;
the clarity of daylight.

Does anyone hold you

in their arms, gently as a sleeping child;
in the morning light, praising all your being?
Do they believe that in your last leaving,
a part of them goes, too? Good. Good. It's true.

Should anyone keep you against your will,
I hope that you can find the strength
inside you to struggle and break free.
Find a soft space and stretch to your full length.

Unfurl the you that loves you most of all.
As I do. As you must know.

If anyone holds you

more faithfully in their heart, I concede:
give them all your roses and let me bleed.
I think this may not happen in our time.
My love has overrun these broken lines.

Three

Infelix Dido

You took our life so lightly for some play's sake
destroyed all the love and grace we made,
and left no trace of history's intimacies.

Deny this, too, but I saw your beauty in the bath;
I sponged your back. I know the fragile parts of you
that don't come easily to light.

You created this—this bearable break between us.

When we were fresh in love,
drenched in sex, you told me about that day
you found her poem, The Queen of Carthage.

Someone held a page open next to you, on the subway,
just long enough for you to grasp. You needed me
to understand what those words meant.

The Wild Iris had already claimed me.
We shared that hunger for fate's imaginings:
poetry of love and loss.

How tragic, and at what cost?

Tonight, the poet is dead. Only you
could know what that means to me.
But we don't speak.

Drowning (Narcissus)

I've become an echo of an echo
in our home. You were everywhere:
being overbearing, boring
into thoughts and space, singing
to a glorious choir only you
could hear.
How do I
swim
this
new
silence?
You took
the coasters
the teaspoons
and left only what didn't shine
back at you. You took until
I gasped, awakened, face-down
in my pond. Mine.
Reflections have a way of claiming,
blurring, and distorting. Oh, but I—
I did love you.

Myriad Pleasures, Denied, While Loving You

Honey mustard dressing: an abomination,
according to you. Olive Garden restaurants: forbidden,
even in name. (Have you ever tasted the pillowing
comfort of those soft, warm breadsticks?)

The ease of family gatherings. The joy of spontaneous
play with a child. The unplanned afternoon or evening's
cozy cocoon. Deep kisses and full body flesh on flesh.
Post-orgasmic intimate breaths. Music. Laughter. Peace.

Scented candles. Everyday fresh flowers. Friendships that bloom
into poetry. Poetry, inhabiting this body, a sacred dance with
    nature.
Deep healing sleep. All the shades in blue.

Silence. Desire. A witnessing and an answering.
My voice. My art. My song. The best seat. The belief
that I belong to this miraculous world.

Penelope's Understanding

All of that striving, and still
more hurdles. More tests.
Why did I think it would end
at the sight of the familiar
olive tree? No sirens in the wind
to compel me.

Ten years missing:
what was I thinking then?
Not a song. Not a myth.
No one touched me.
A decade at sea, adrift.

Then, the words
returning, weaving:
I am both love's fidelity,
belonging to this soft-
shrouded world, and also
the empty seeker.

I recall the ship, the wave,
that ease of leaving;
the beating of my heart receding.

Basic Algorithm of Time

It's been 215 days since
I learned it was you.

No one more surprised than
my heart—skipping—two beats,
the 24th time I saw your face.

Later, alone, I laughed in disbelief
at the absurdity of my desire.
Still, the tick, tick, ticking

of my relentless heart:
multiplying each conversation
and casual touch;

adding and subtracting
the milliseconds of your attention
canceled by indifference.

Each dawn sings its awakening with your name;
every night falls with reckless dreams
that you will never claim.

The impossible hours lie in between.

Beloved

I must take care not to write
exclusively for you, not to paint
images for your eyes
alone, not to imagine
a home in your soul.
I must be cautious,
and take great care that I
do not love you
in such a reckless, human way.

To a Rock Hound

What is it that you so love
about this crystal? Is it the near-perfect,
highly-ordered, microscopic structure?
Or the way she pulses and dazzles?
Is it the alignment of those atoms
held in your hand? The motif of
intermolecular forces of attraction?
The thrill of sharp edges and glacial striations?
Does the ambiguity of her deep clarity
excite your thoughts? Do you imagine
her birth and history, who might have held her
before your claim? Is it sweeter in darkness
to dream of her fiery glow or to caress her
surfaces boldly at dawn? Perhaps you love her
without knowing how your love is returned:
in tender reflection, in the refraction of pure light.
If only I, too, were made of stone

.

Four

The Child Not Taken

(after Frost)

Two beds remain in my childhood room,
And thinking now of that distant past
And meager space of such cold and gloom
Or all the dreams since come to ruin,
I see those beds in a different cast.

My sister's bed hugged the farthest wall;
My own huddled near the open door
Where footsteps creaked from stair to hall
As shadows lengthened, at last, to fall
Upon her sleeping, dreamless form.

And both of us defenseless lay
In sheets of pink no stain had marred.
Oh, I was spared for another day.
But knowing now how debts are paid,
I find myself as damaged, cold, and hard.

When no one else can hear my cries
I tell the story of our small fears:
Two beds were in our childhood, and I—
I kept my silence. I sleep with lies;
And that will haunt me all my years.

Still Life

No matter what age you find,
the yo-yo string unwinds
to its full length.
The striped top spins
an angry thrum; vibrates
in your hand.

Unreel backward
toward those days
you could have lived
without meaning to recall.

Your father's first slap
echoes like a pebble
falling in a canyon
inside the desert
of your small self.

Holy Week

(the wolf also shall dwell with the lamb)

All that week she held his promise near;
worried the smooth round bead of hope,
while waiting for the slow-moving school bus
or deciphering the world after Dick and Jane.

In a world of shining, immaculate girls,
she alone bore a dark seed at her center,
which she imagined would scatter—
like dandelion fluff—at the slightest breath of God.

She prayed, she prayed, day into night
to receive the sacred message;
words redemptive with mystery,
engraved on tissue-paper-thin skin.

At six, she learned that evil exists
companion to her own desire.

She kept their pact for years,
though he had failed to keep his word

and Easter morning found her
with nothing holy in her hands,
still sitting on his filthy knee.

Early Lessons

My teacher's unspoken poem landed—
a small bird in my throat. I knew
without knowing, what was appropriate to say
and what could never be revealed.

When she did speak, reciting,
"Hope is the thing with feathers,"
a wild flutter ripped
her voice through me.

A guarded thing—her dark brown
eyes took me deep into the forest
where brilliant plumes of yearning
spilled from her thoughts to mine. She was quiet—
She was mad—She rarely smiled—She knew me.

Lessons in Care

My mother practiced injecting oranges
during those first weeks of nursing school.

Neighbors whispered, “How strange,
she’s raised five children,

all on her own, and isn’t that enough
caretaking for any woman?”

She told me hospital stories
of the big, bearded man who cried

as she gently sponged his wounds;
and the fragile gray husk of a woman

who pleaded daily for nothing more
than someone to brush her hair.

My mother touched her, with tenderness,
and Elsie sang, “Let me call you sweetheart.”

    The hardest thing, she once confessed
    was learning to cut someone deliberately:

    a quick slice of the finger,
    a necessary bloodletting.

Years later, I think of this
and wonder exactly what she’s taught me.

Always the strong one, I do what’s needed:
cut you, quickly, decisively—and I bleed.

Danville

My sister is slowly dying in the town where we were born.

When I visit, she wants a chili dog from the Wiener Works, and
so I go,
shielding myself from the harsh sunlight and mid-day blight of
Danville.

I want to argue, to point out that nitrates are harmful to her
health,
but everyone I know is sick or dying in this town:
tumors on the spine, cancer in the brain and colon.

The street signs declare this a famous place: the hometown
of Bobby Short, Gene Hackman, and the Van Dyke brothers.
Now famously number one on the EPA's list for toxic zinc levels;
nitrates seem a silly concern. We lucky ones moved on.

I drive my rental car through the empty streets
seeking the public library and those sister
lionesses flanking the entry; those beautiful beasts
who soothed me and sparked my dreams.
They seem unconcerned that the sanctuary of my youth
is now a war museum.

War Museum: those difficult letters burn
in orange and neon blue. The way I choose to live
strange and bright, away from you.

Danville, Again

The truth lives on in a small-town
bullseye, where I play darts with the locals.
No wine or beer on tap, only spirits, and Solo cups
on the bar for spitting tobacco juice. I lose
myself here in this town; every time I return,
I become someone past. A quiet girl,
an accident, a tiny blunder. There is no light
for me here, no way of keeping clear.
I left early, and I never looked back. But the pull—
the singular arc—the draw—of family and history—
is confounding. I can’t unimagine myself
from the punctured, wounded center of here.

Five

Art of Deception

Kanazawa, Ishikawa, Japan:
21st Century Museum of Contemporary Art

We go down, down, to the bottom
of the swimming pool:
the illusion of water, a trick of light.
Gobsmacked as only tourists
could be, seeing as children once more,
we walk the floor like dumb crustaceans
in our somber black coats and clumsy boots.

The two young geishas in kimonos
are a field of chrysanthemums
and poppies exploding against
the false blue depths.

The beautiful girls are startling
as birds in their red yukatas, yet invisible
in their scripted roles. I see the intimacy
of their twined gaze, reflecting a desire
to be seen and known in the open air.

Back at the ryokan, we put on
matching yukatas before the kaiseki meal.
Two white girls mirroring the narrative arc:
everything in season; a tasting of delicacies
fleeting as love on the tongue.

Isis Laments

(for Jim, August 1990)

The fiercely pretty men
gather in blank corridors
near your hospital bed,
compelled to witness
their own impending tragedy.

You leave and they take
your political posters,
your purple feather boa.

Your lover inherits old books,
worn blue paisley sheets,
a surly cat named Alabaster.

An old friend carries on;
a conversation you began
but never meant to finish.

I travel the night
grasping at pieces of you
falling from the broken sky.

Caretaker's Lament

If the prickly pear
wants to die,

I swear, I will let it.
No more pruning
interventions,
watering
schedules, or slow
drip of meds.

I am done
with that kind of life.

Held in containers,
coddled indoors. No.

I am freeing those roots.

Let them sigh

from the compost heap, creeping

fingers thrust
deep into the dark, crumbling earth.

Let them find the company of worms
vastly better than this

wasted time with me.

The Numbers

January 2002

The city was still a wound;
her dark streets gaping with the lack
of crowds streaming—people
heading somewhere exciting or mundane.
No traffic howls or beeps. Just silence.
The emptied streets held huge traffic cones
and caution tape, redirecting familiar crosstown routes.

I remember steam rising from the centers
of the Avenues. Could that have been true?
The silent subway grates echoed
each day's uncertainty and fear.
Flowers strewn on concrete. Posters on every
available space showed faces
of the missing—*the missing*—as yet not dead.

Candles burned that night I met you
in the mournful city. I brought you home
and we made our bodies a safe, sacred space
away from that eerie glow. We fell into love
within the shadow of those bodies falling
from the towers. We fell into the immenseness
of a collective, exponential grief.

Days of red wine and comfort food
numbed the pain and put band-aids
on those irreversible scars. But the stars—
the stars were no longer the light we knew:
they were grief candles burning holes
through the endless dark.

The Numbers

March 2020

The darkness descended again in the spring.
Green grasses and delicate flowers,
absurd and obscene, next to the bodies
piled up in the streets, in containers, awaiting
mass burials. The daily death count:
black numbers in a guessing game.
Fear and uncertainty crept over the city
like a familiar shadow, raged
against us in our comfort zone.
We washed our hands until they chafed;
sanitized our groceries—our home—our needs—
not knowing how the virus could come.
A wound was awakened in us:
torn open by the witnessing of horrors again.
For two years, we held vigil against
the plague. Then we fell apart
as other loved ones, isolated in hospital beds,
were cleaved. I never thought
that we too, would become a statistic.

The Cloisters

Beneath bell-toned hours,
your laugh invades clear spaces,
a ghost note. In the garden,
you flutter among the living
on dark, spiraling wings.

Inside the cool, dank rooms,
a procession of saints and martyrs
in miniature, mementos of carved wood,
hold swords of toothpick scale.

I imagine layers of shavings curled,
exquisite mounds on the stone floor
as the essential is revealed.

This grievous work of letting go
moves slow, and slower still,

quiets the pulse of the sun's inward turning.

How we demand this stripping bare,
this painful surrender to loss,
through which we discover
our human form, wooden heart intact.

A Retiring of Sorts

You can fish in the Loxahatchee River.
At least, that's what I tell myself
this morning, in bed and worrying
the daylight that won't cast,

the migrant bird songs that won't last
when my neighbor's pool pump grinds to life.
I'm going to be all right. Today,
that's what I tell myself—a shiny lie.

A life in retrospect is always wrong:
too many bad turns and half-hearted starts.
I tell myself jokes to pass the time.
I listen to the wind chimes—a gentle tolling.

A choice not made
is still a choice. A dubious distinction
to be laid to rest with me, I hope.

I hope. I do. Isn't that amazing?
After all the truths I've known,
how have I flown from there
to wither here in this Sunshine State?

What a state I'm in today. What a state.

Future Forecast

Now   I am older   I have time to imagine
the deepest thoughts of birds   the starling's sad longing
for home   shadows
each murmuration like a descant thunderstorm.

But   I should say   starlings' thought   for their mind is a single
beat   multiplied   by wing-dark   design   to confuse
the falcon.   Why   do I dream of this   lifting uprush
thunderous clapping   as though it is my pulse?

Why   does the cardinal arrive   majestic every day
to watch me, watching him   from inside my cage?
The black mask   can't disguise   his disdain
for the rule of man, or for me trapped in my poems.

Now and then I see a congregation of Ibis
walking down the street. Egyptian gods of writing
yet, they don't have much to say, these days
in Florida   last to leave   before the storm
tell me   we've seen   these hurricanes before.

Every Woman Knows

In the first dream, a man enters the ladies'
room of a public building where I am alone.
I try to tell him politely that he isn't allowed—
but he cuts me off with, "My choice." When I protest,
he gives me that look and says, "Your body—My choice,"
and my animal brain scurries in the way every woman knows:
How far to the door? If I scream, will anyone hear?
Should I bargain or fight?

When I wake up, my heart can't quiet, and my mind won't stop
thinking about the dangers of a straight man in any room.
In my bathroom, my gynecologist's exam room, my bedroom
(which is erased in the classroom, where we don't say "gay"
and I am deleted from the history books).

In the second dream, a man is driving a pickup truck through the
snow;
speeding to frighten me. We're careening out of control,
my two girlfriends trapped in the back seat. He is curious—
an epidemiologist of sin. He wants to know
how many times I've been exposed to gay sex.

When I wake up from this dream; I force myself to stay awake.
I think of a woman I have loved and recall the softness of her
lips and inner thigh. I feel again her tender touch.
And in that place of vulnerability, I find my strength.

Six

Epiphany

I relinquish my desire
to write the perfect poem.
No more straining to describe
the exquisite dance of starlings;
or the unfolding of the rarest flower.
No need for political statements;
irrelevant and too late. No failed love
sonnets or gentle aubades.

I will bury my words:
ferment them in rich soil,
entomb them like a saint.
Those nouns and softening
sounds will make friends
with the endless night.
The inchoate.

When the perfect poem
rises, offering itself to me,
I will place it tenderly
on the clean white sheet
and give praise.

Made in United States
Orlando, FL
30 July 2025

63387522R00037